Bear

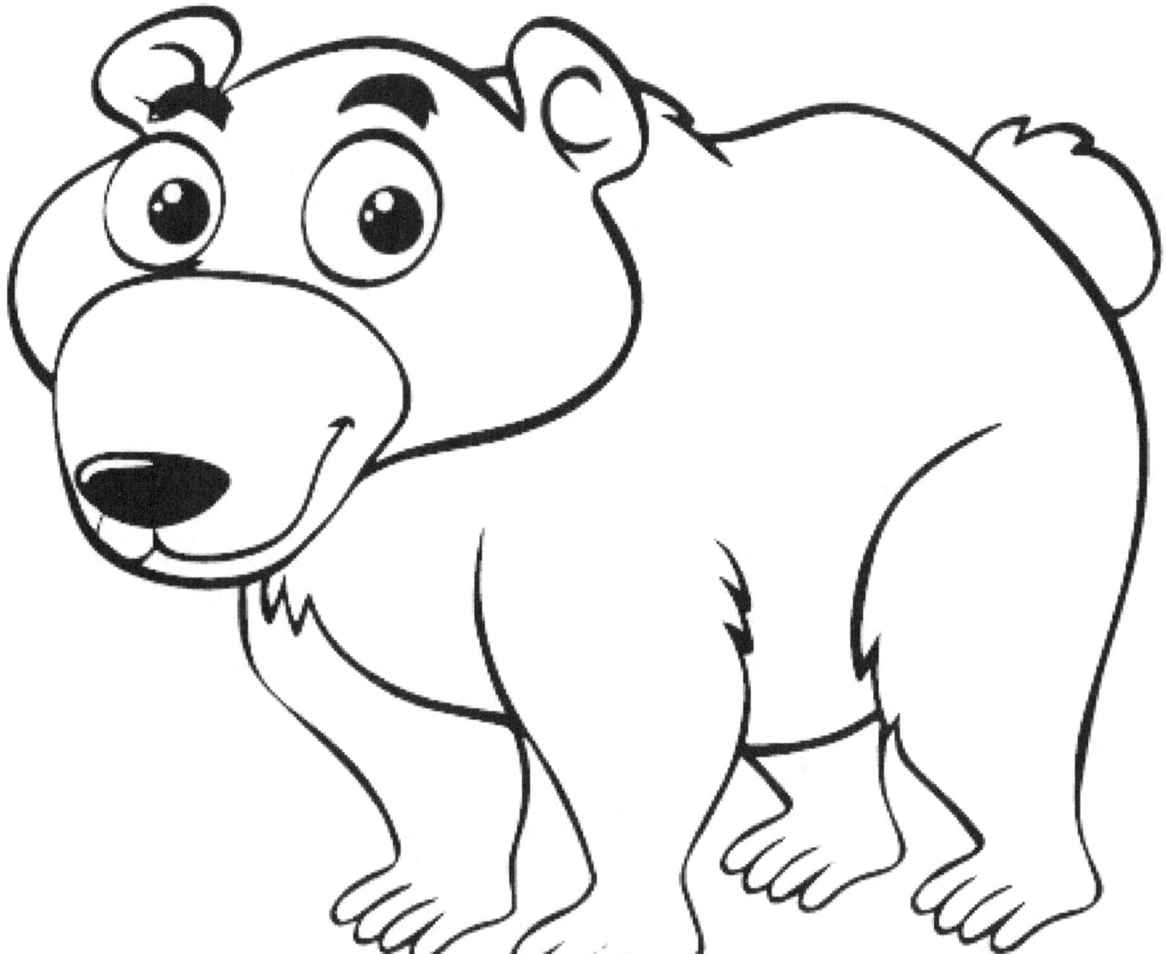

1

ONE

Lamb

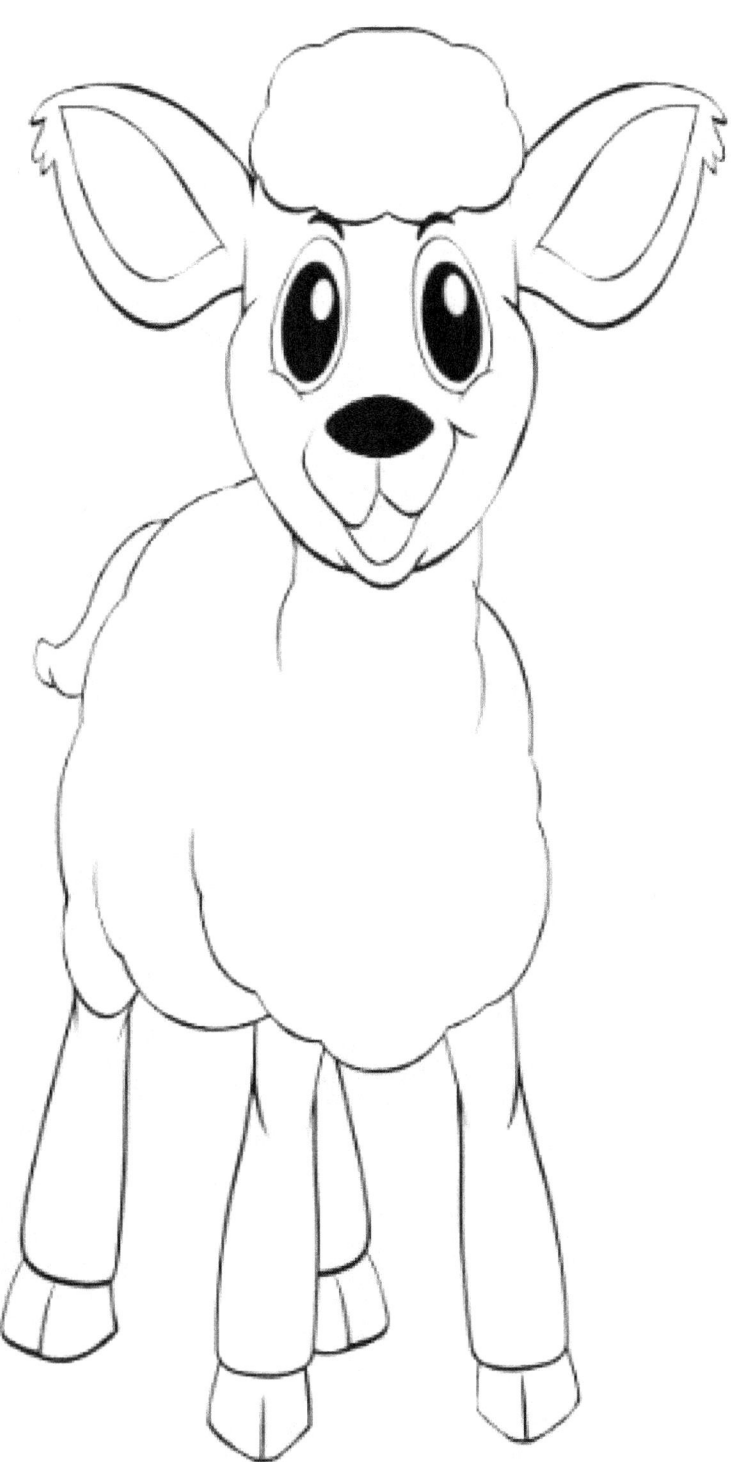

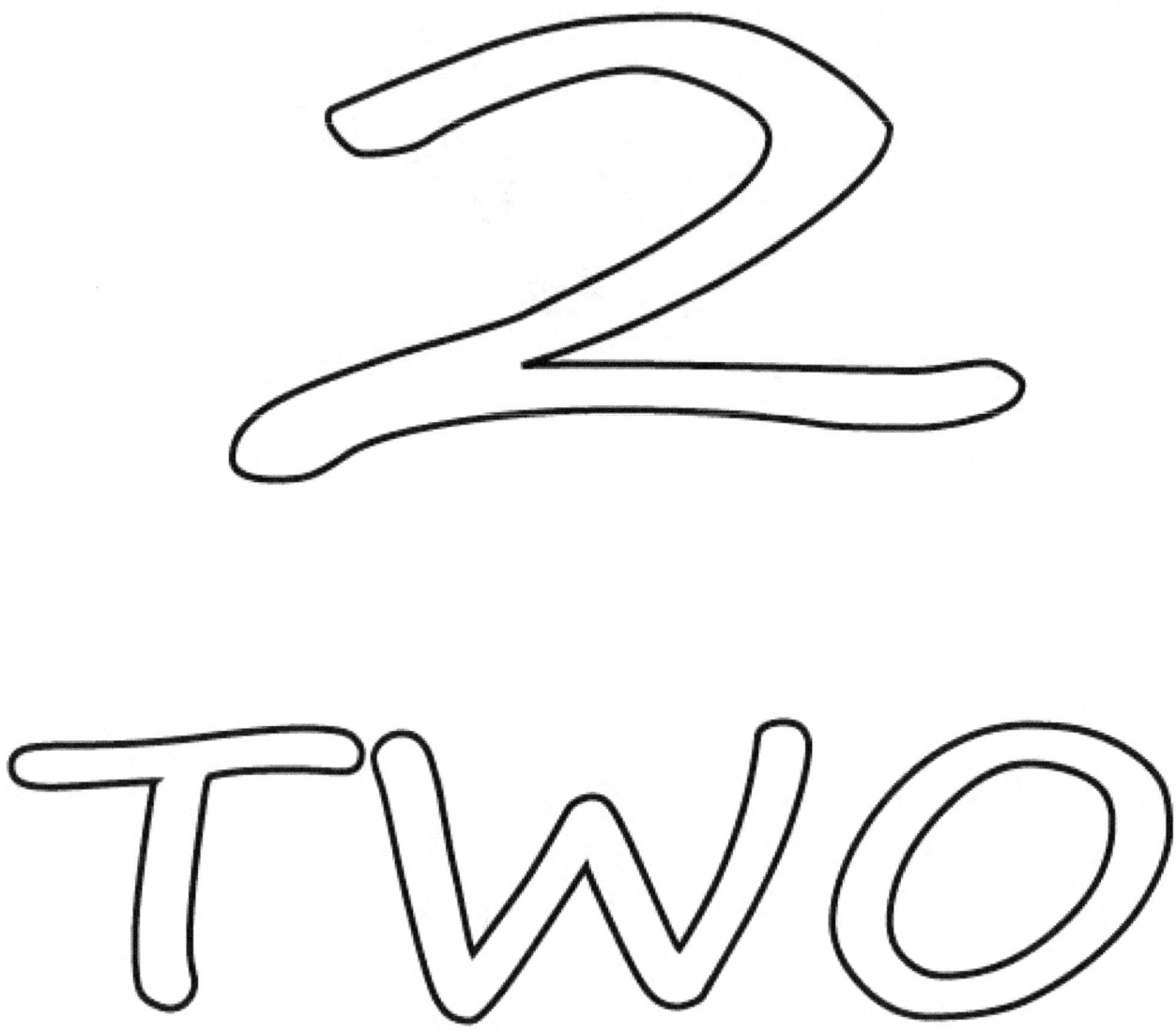

bunny

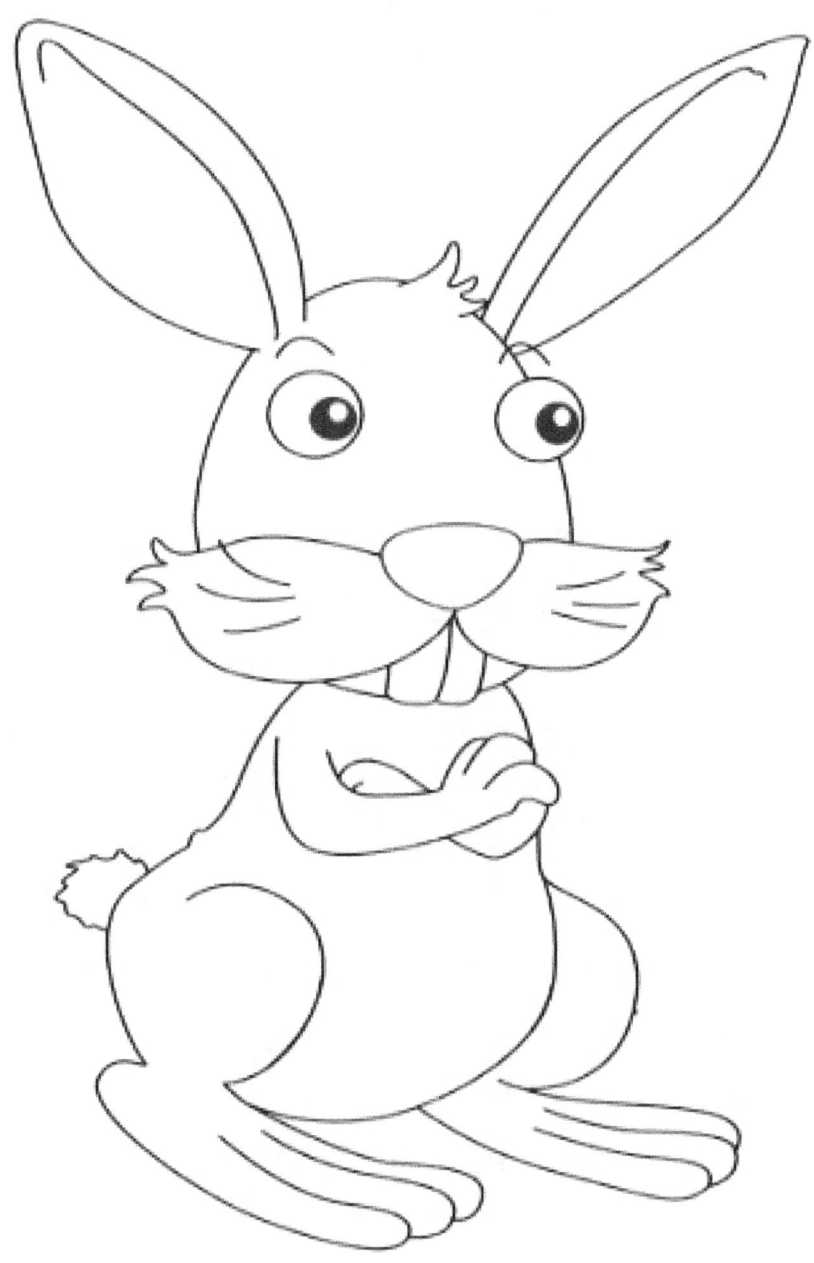

3

THREE

kitten

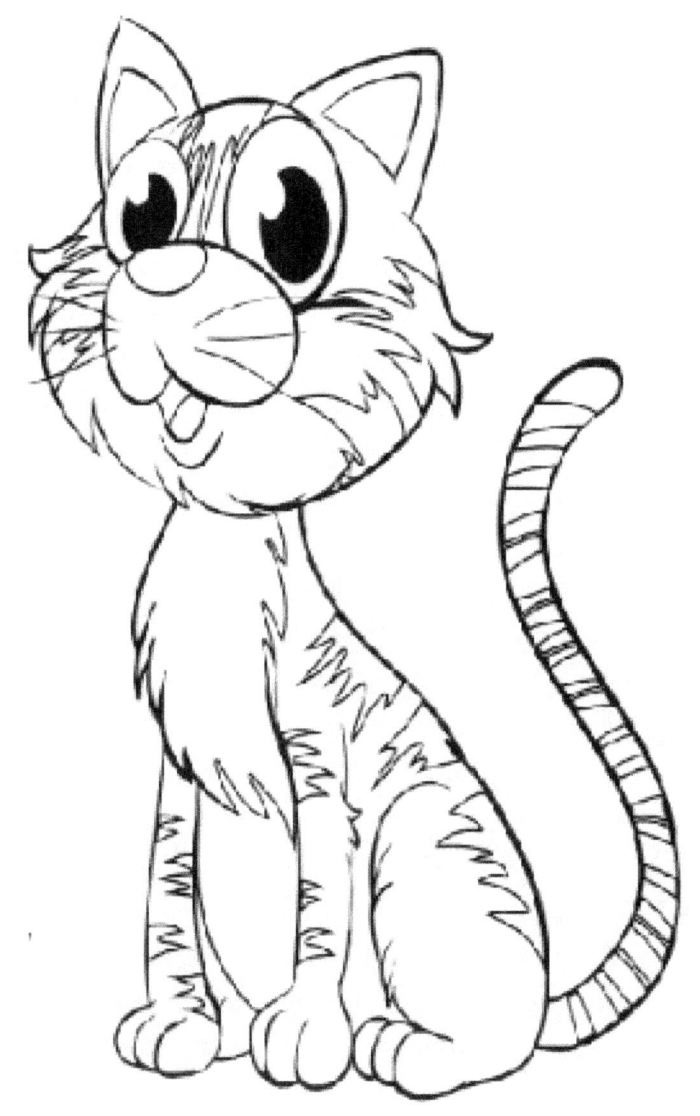

4

Four

chimpanzee

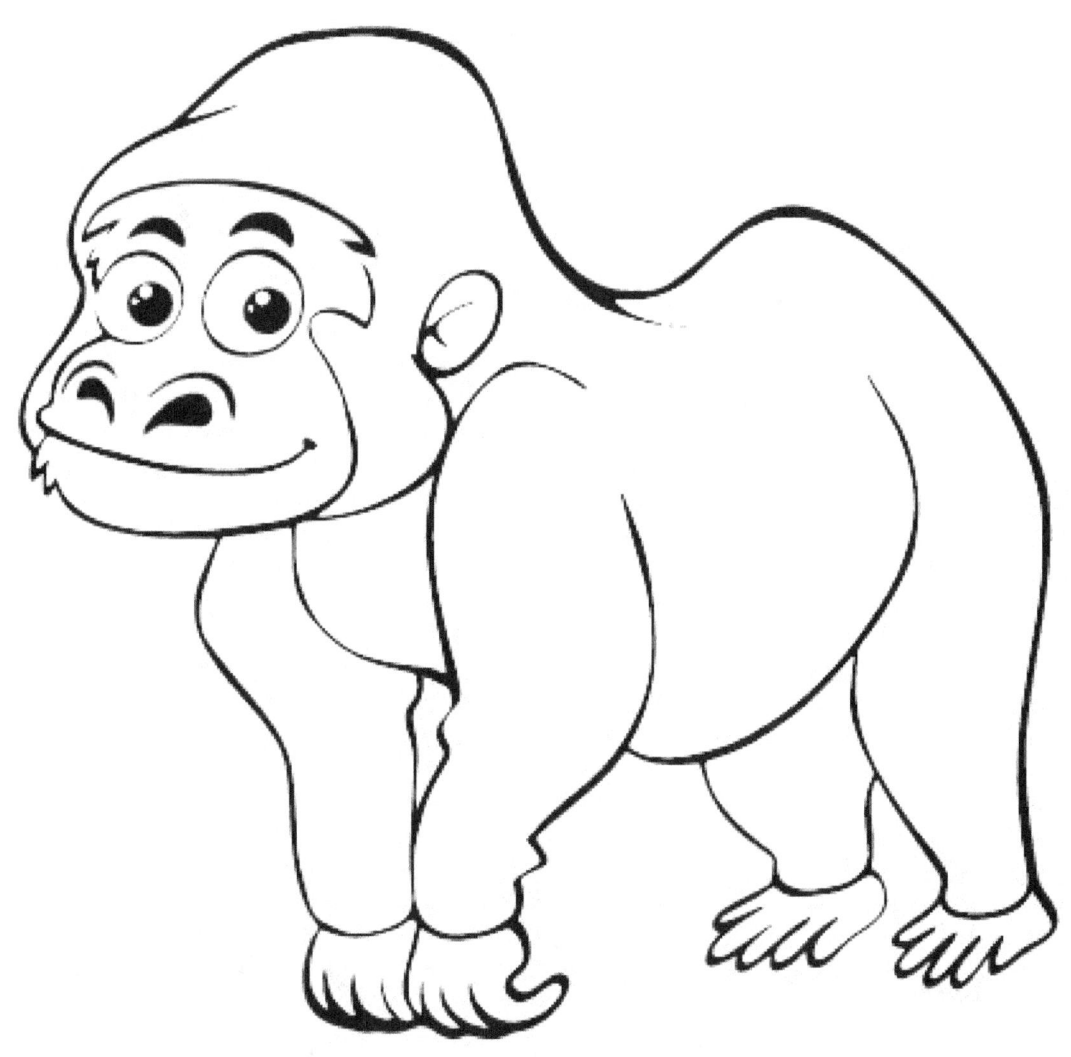

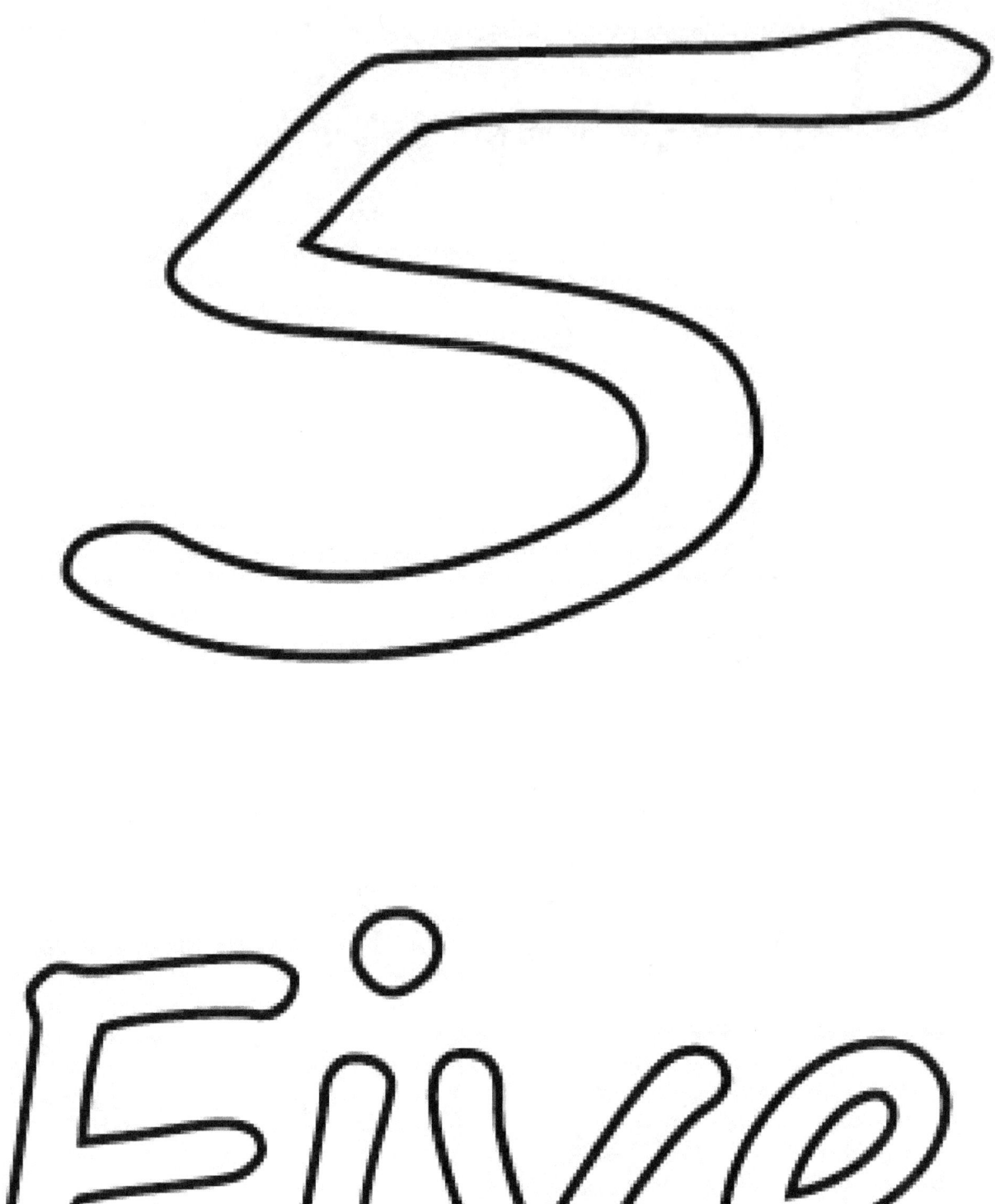

Cheetah

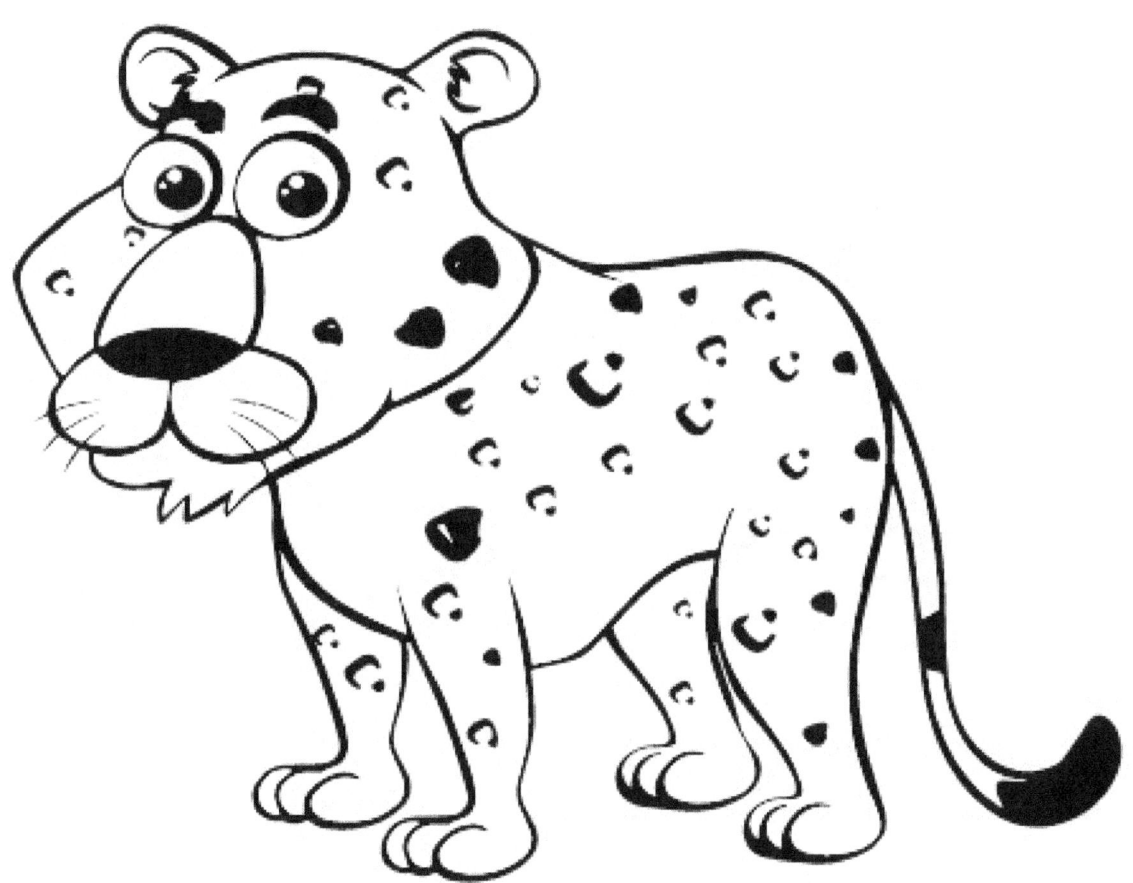

6

six

Elephant

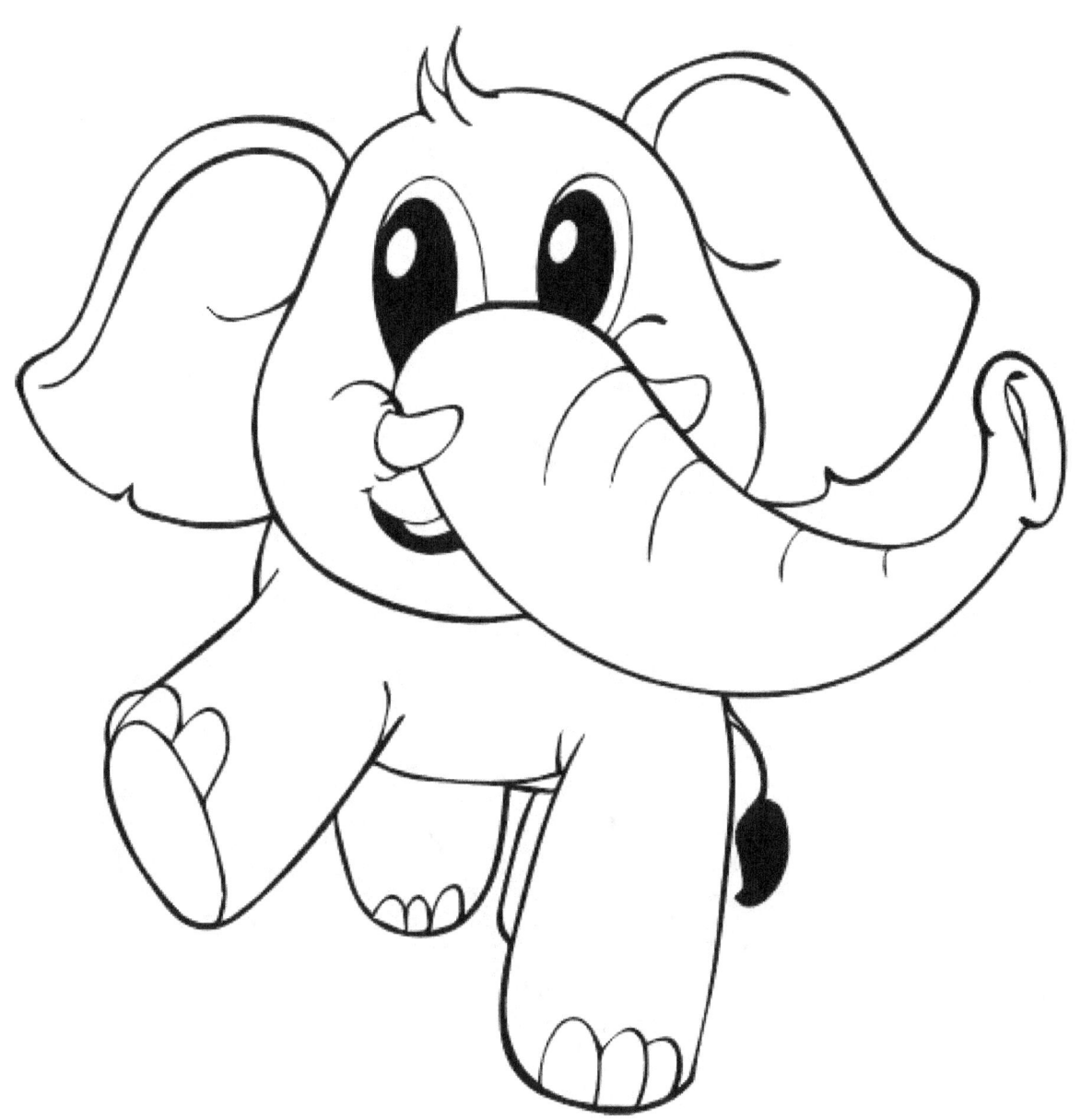

7

Seven

Kitten

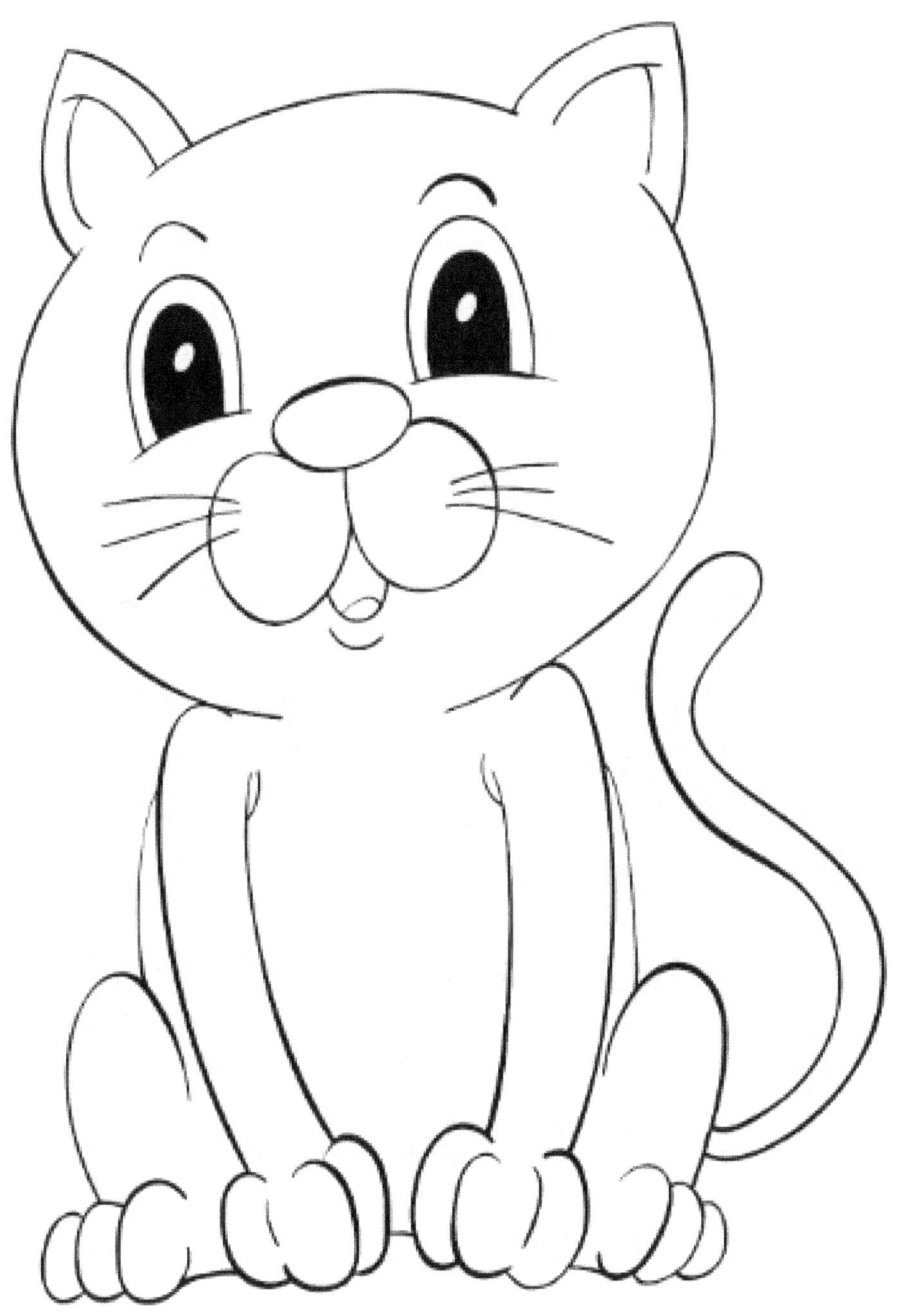

8

Eight

Foal

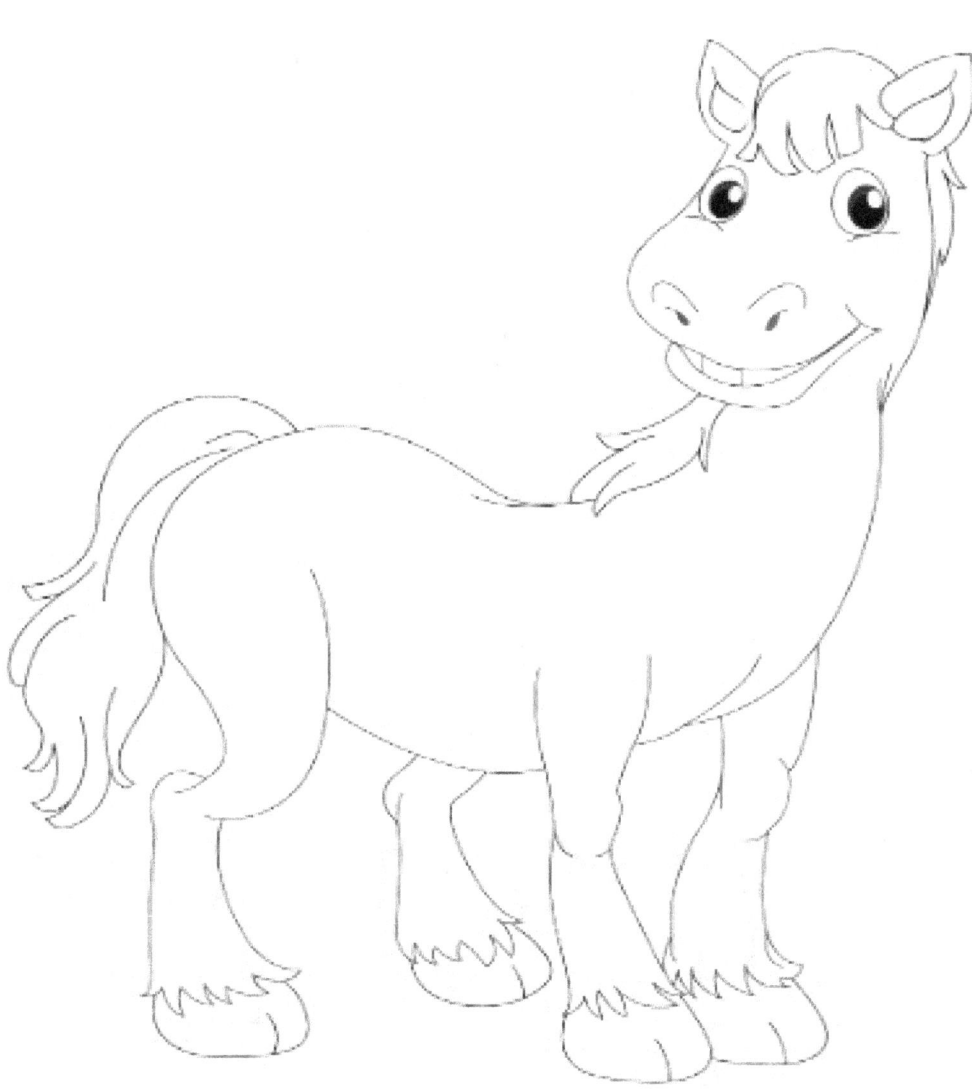

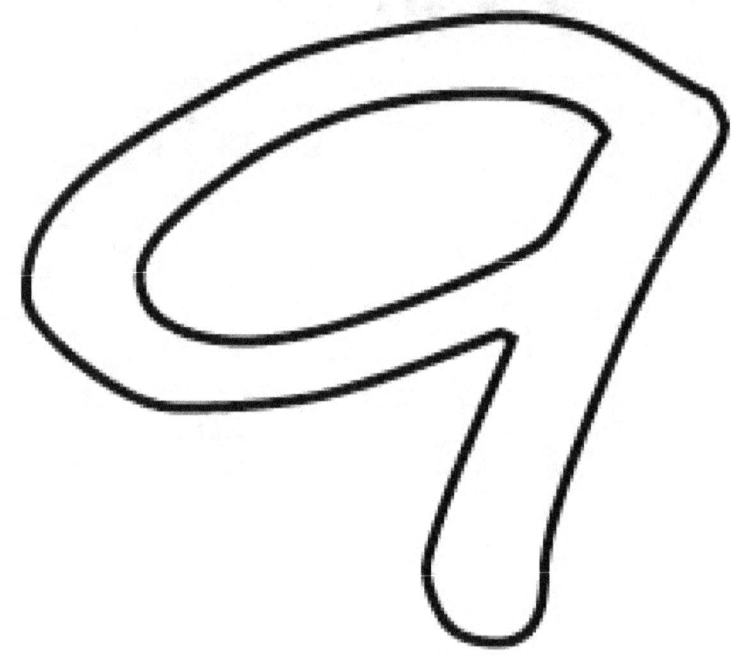

Nine

fawn

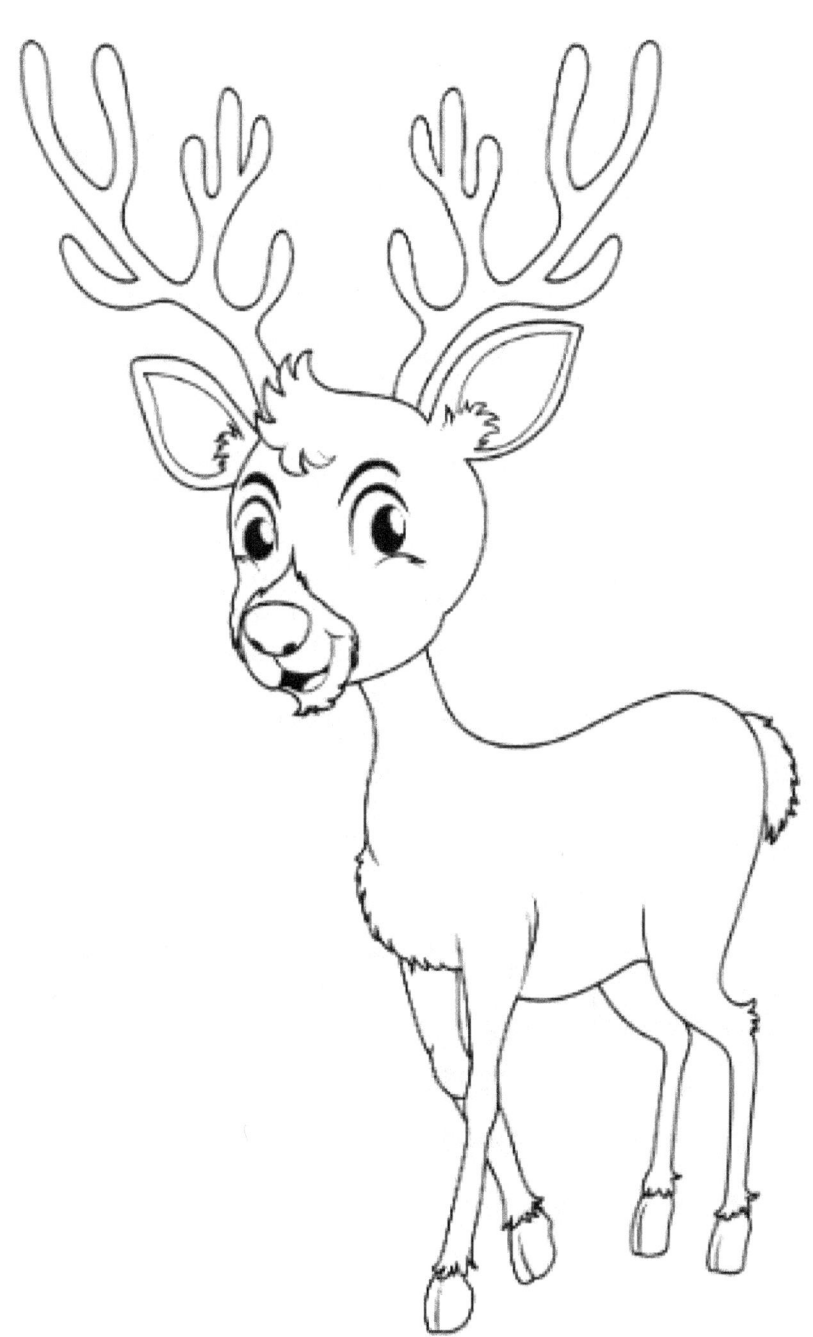

10

Ten

Frog

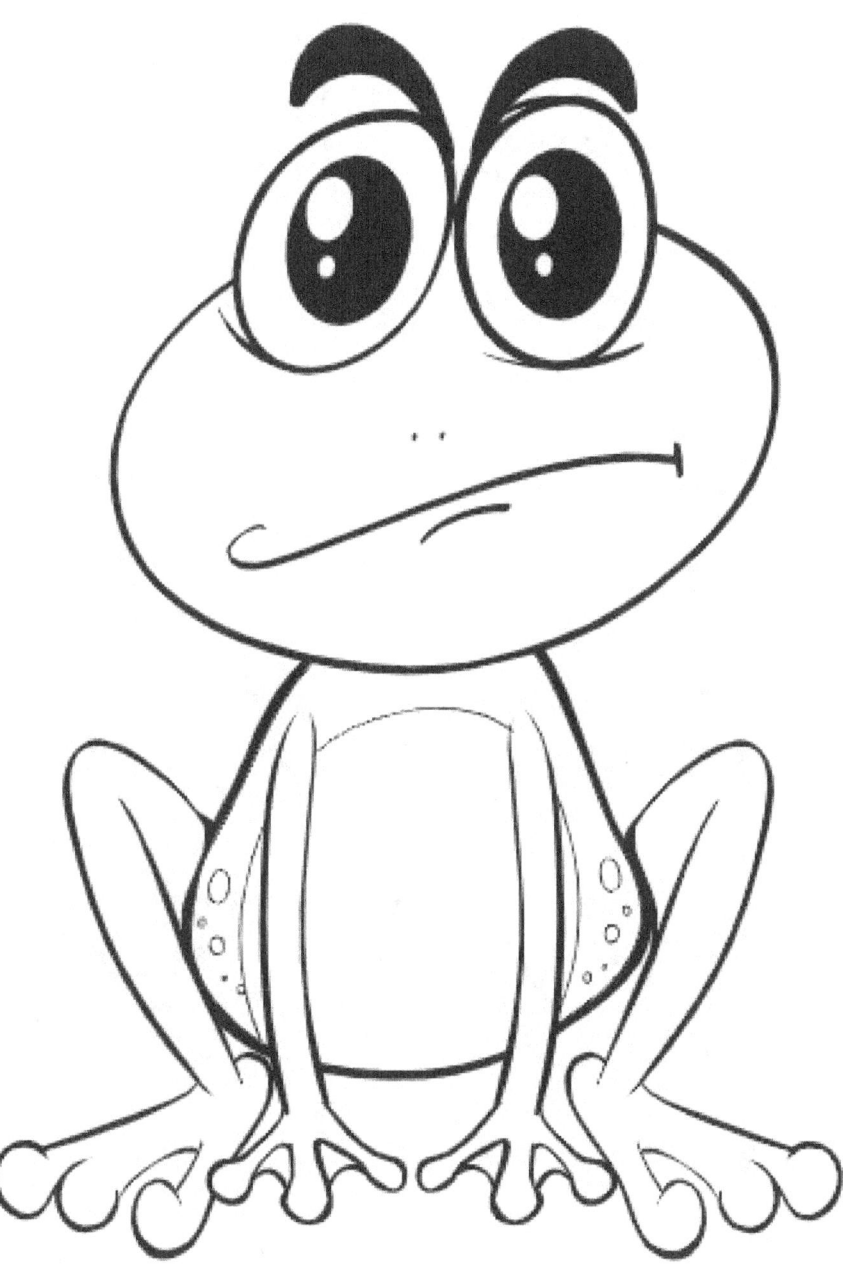

11

Eleven

Puppy

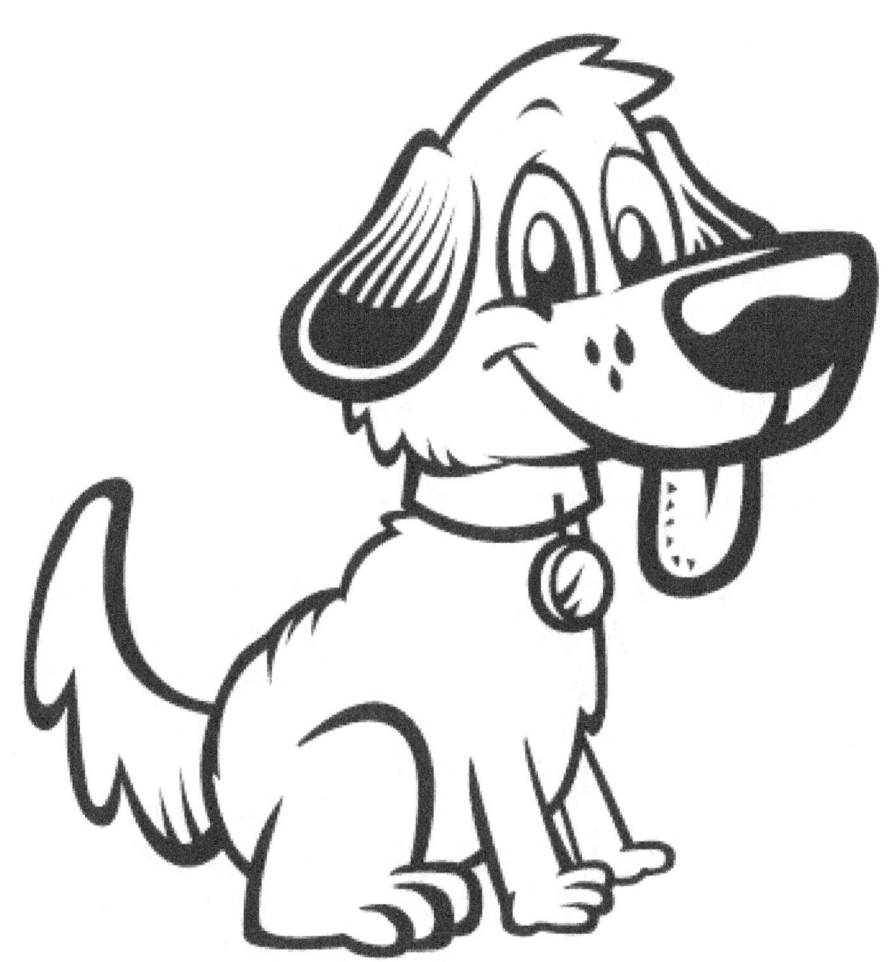

12

Tweleve

Giraffe

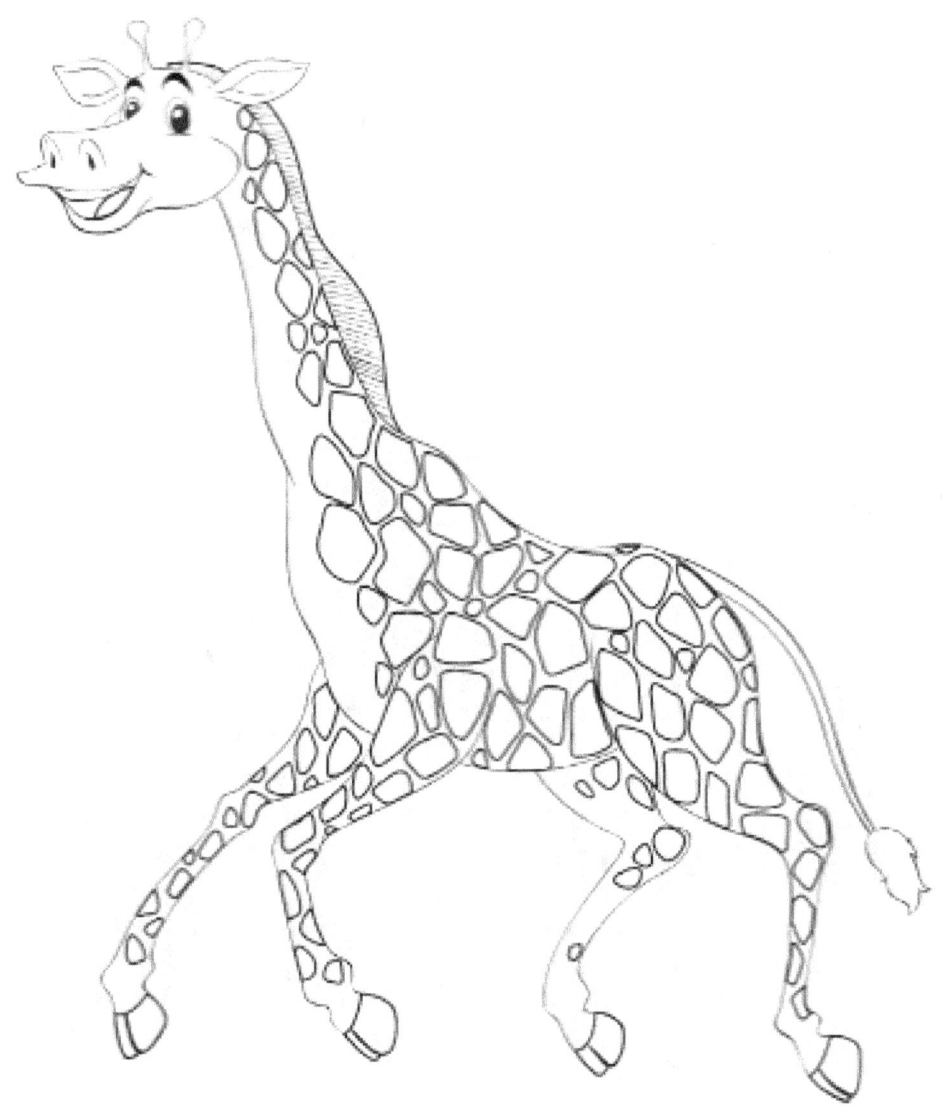

13

Thirteen

Rhinoceros

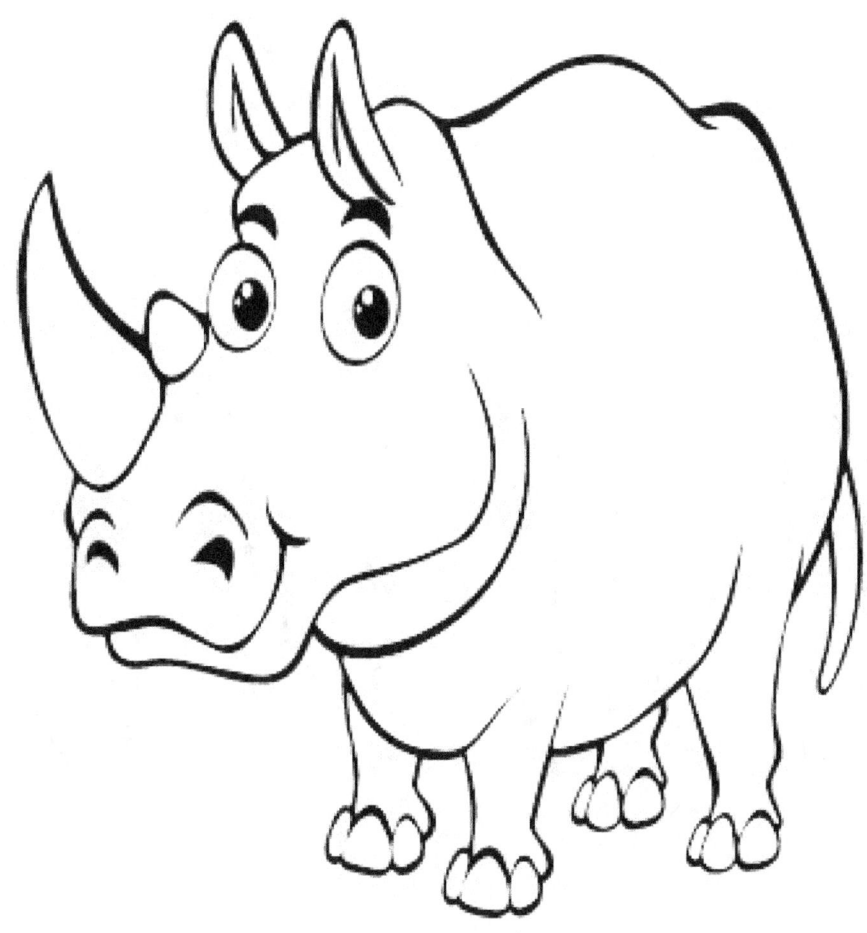

14

Fourteen

bear cub

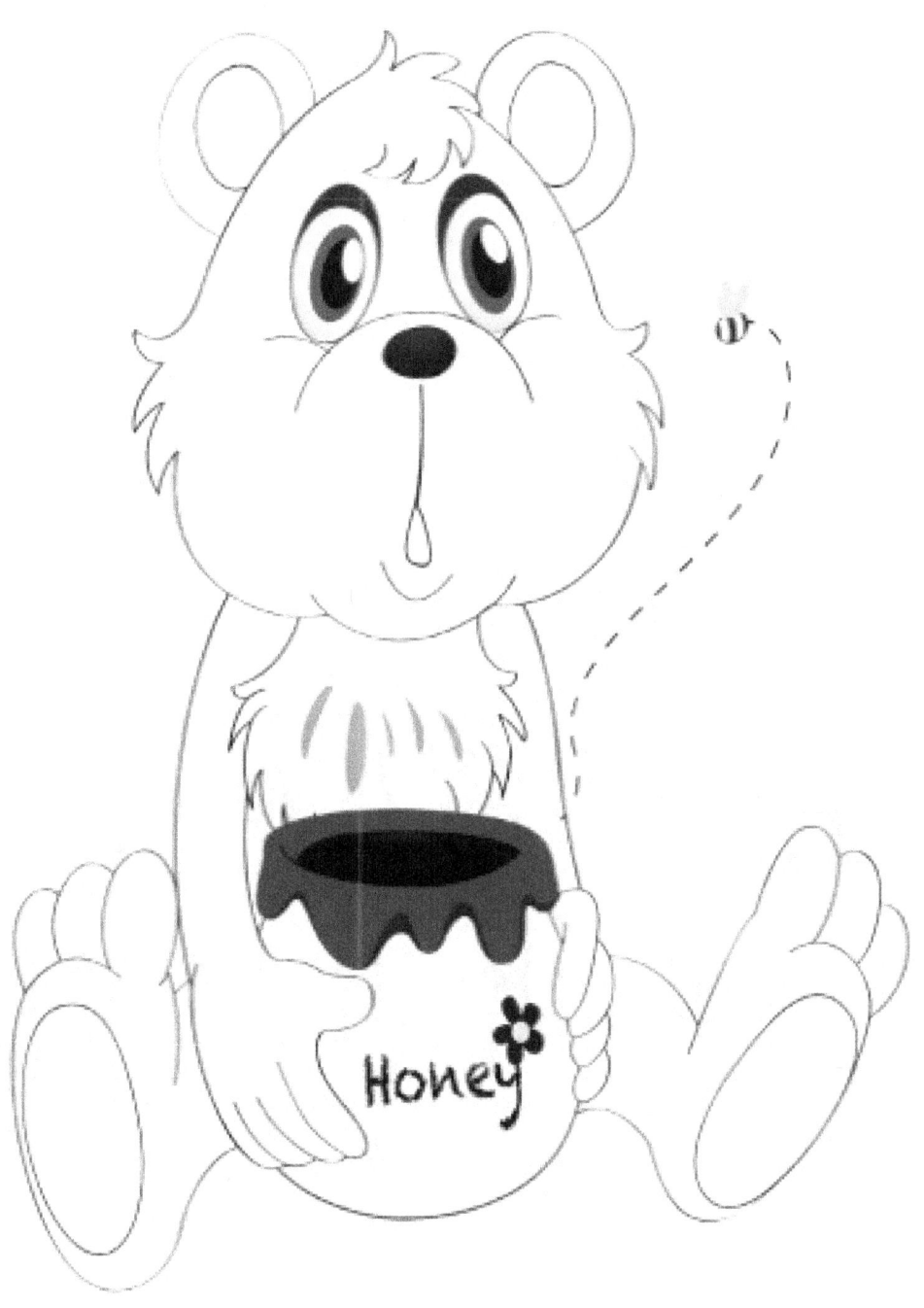

15

Fifteen

hippopotamus

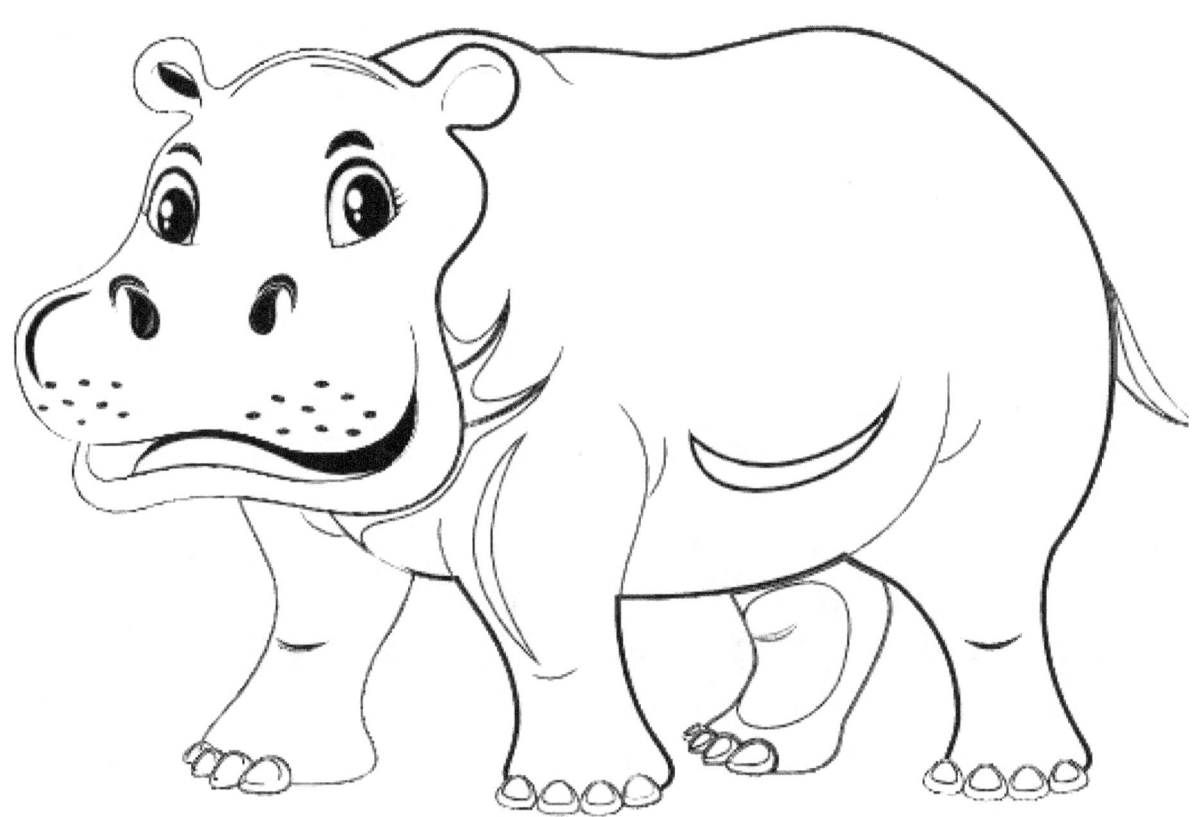

16

Sixteen

Kangaroo

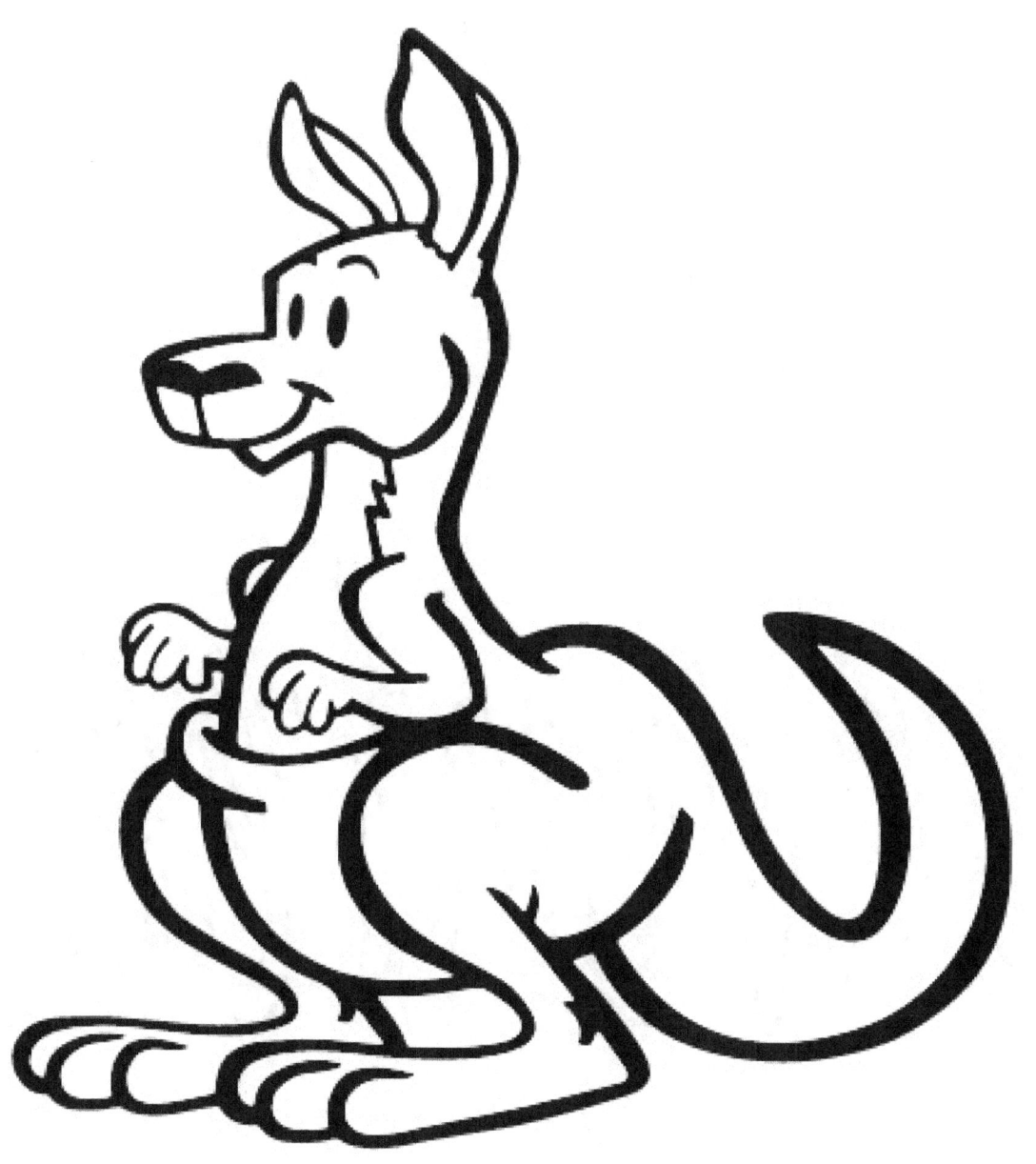

17

Seventeen

Rabbit

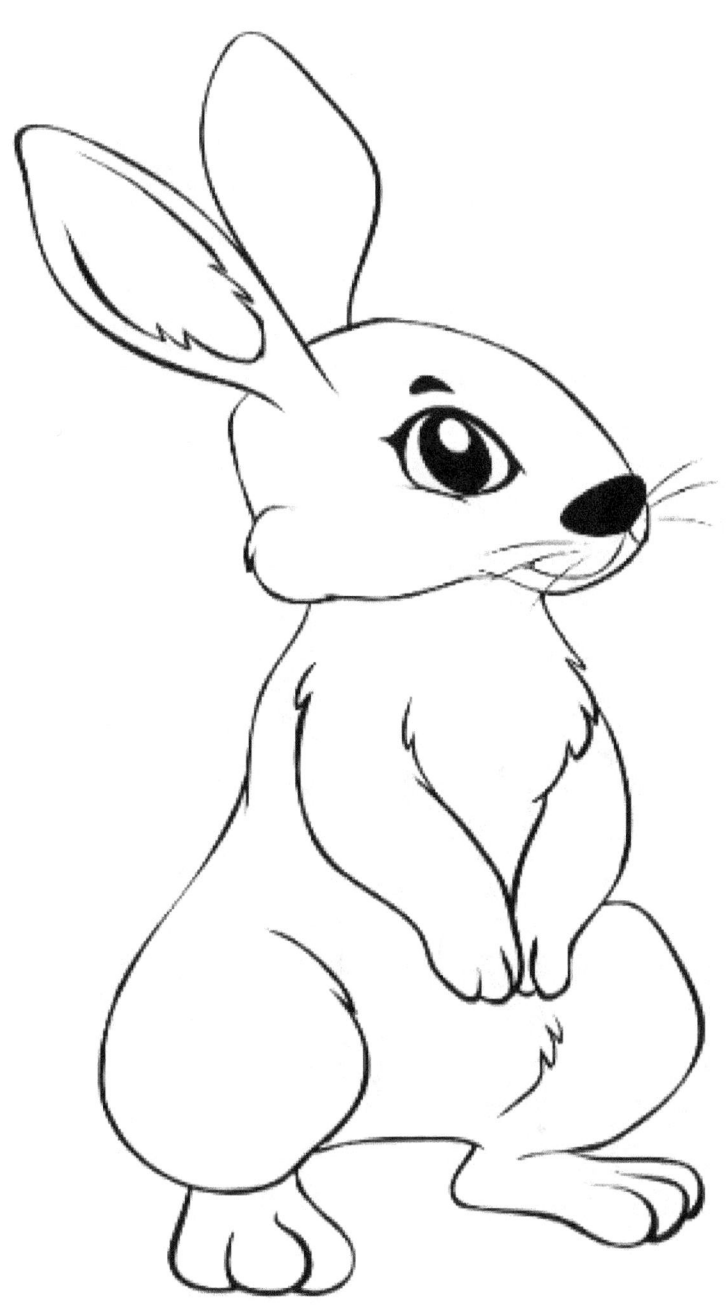

18

Eighteen

Money

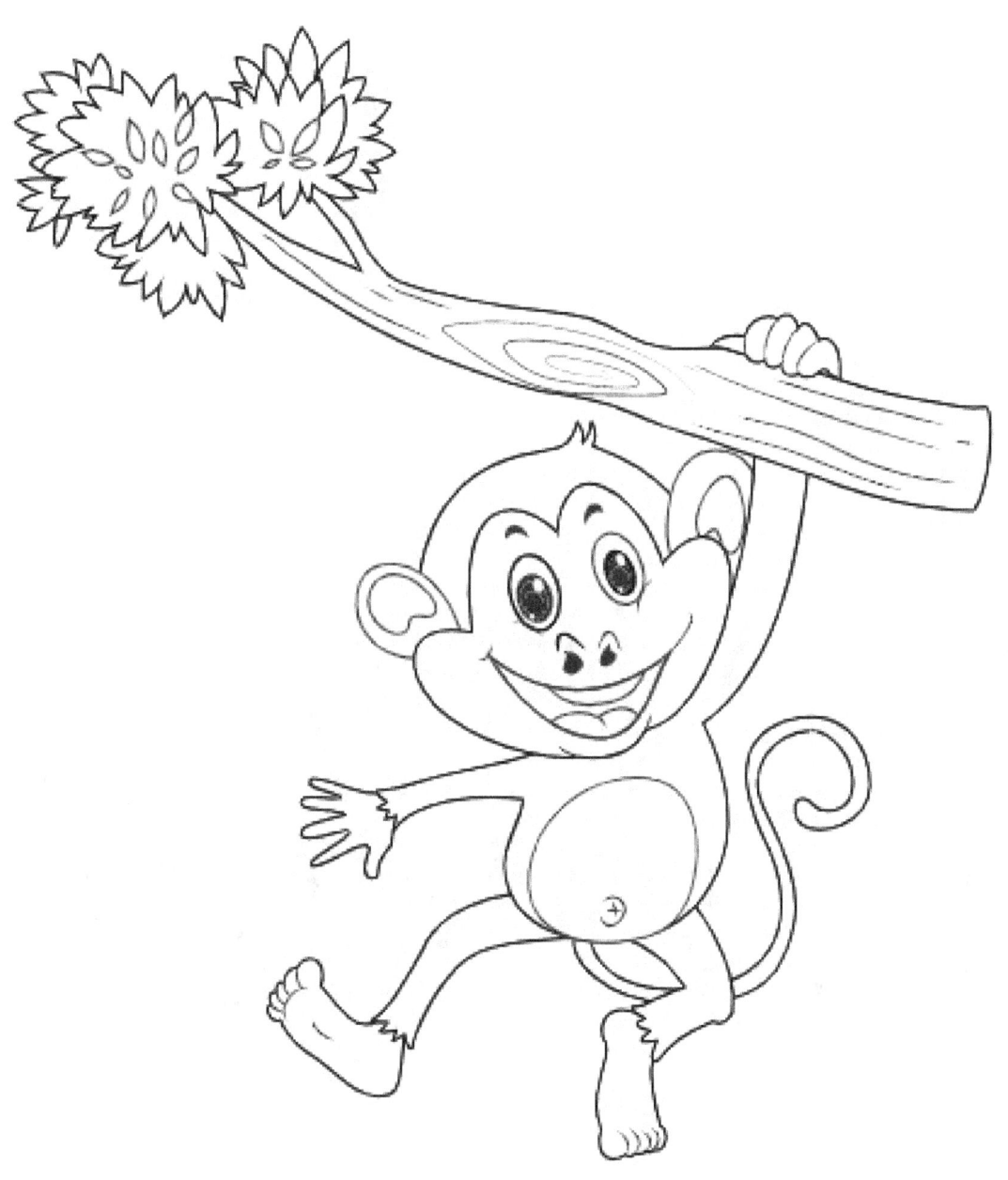

19

Nineteen

Wild boar

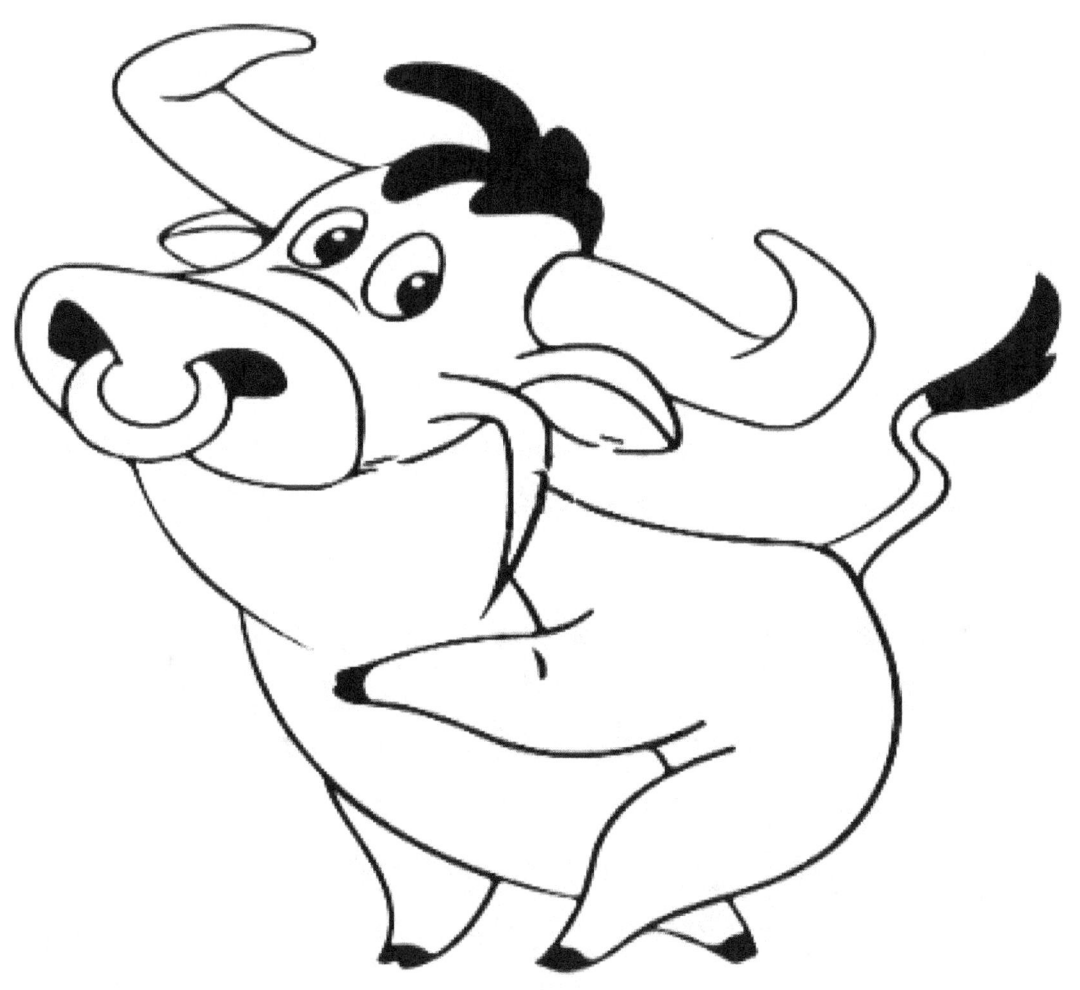

20
Twenty

Rat

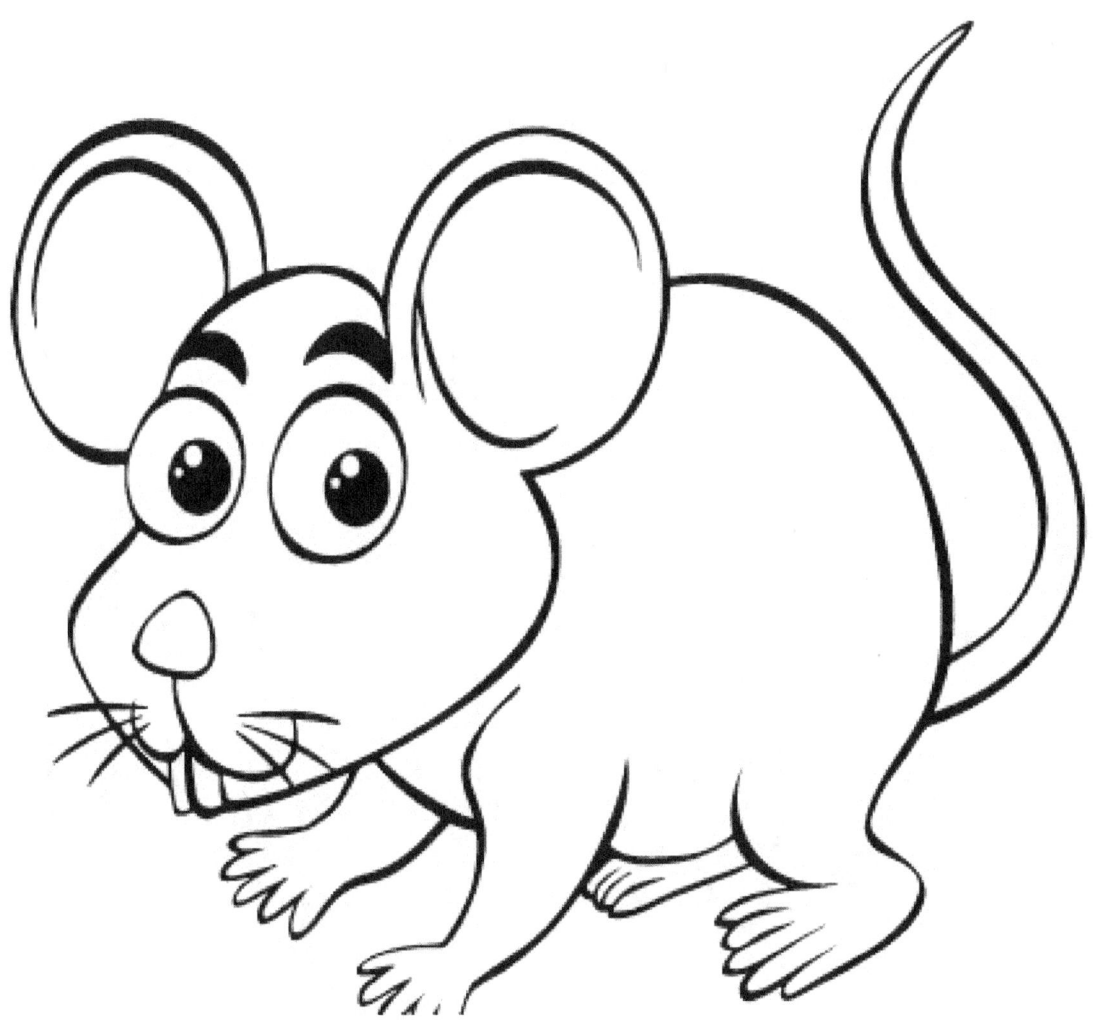

21

Twentyone

Lamb

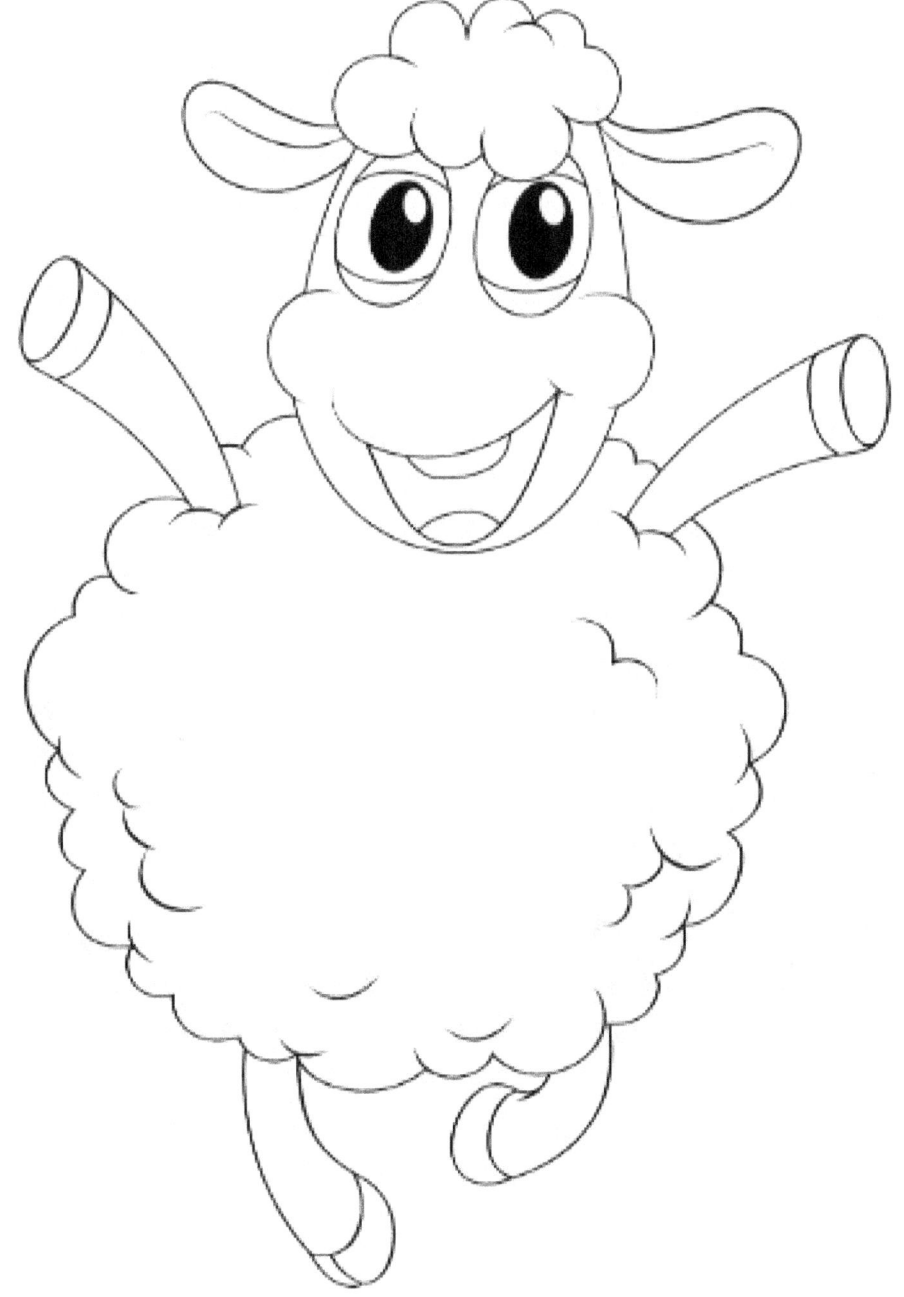

22

Twentytwo

Tiger

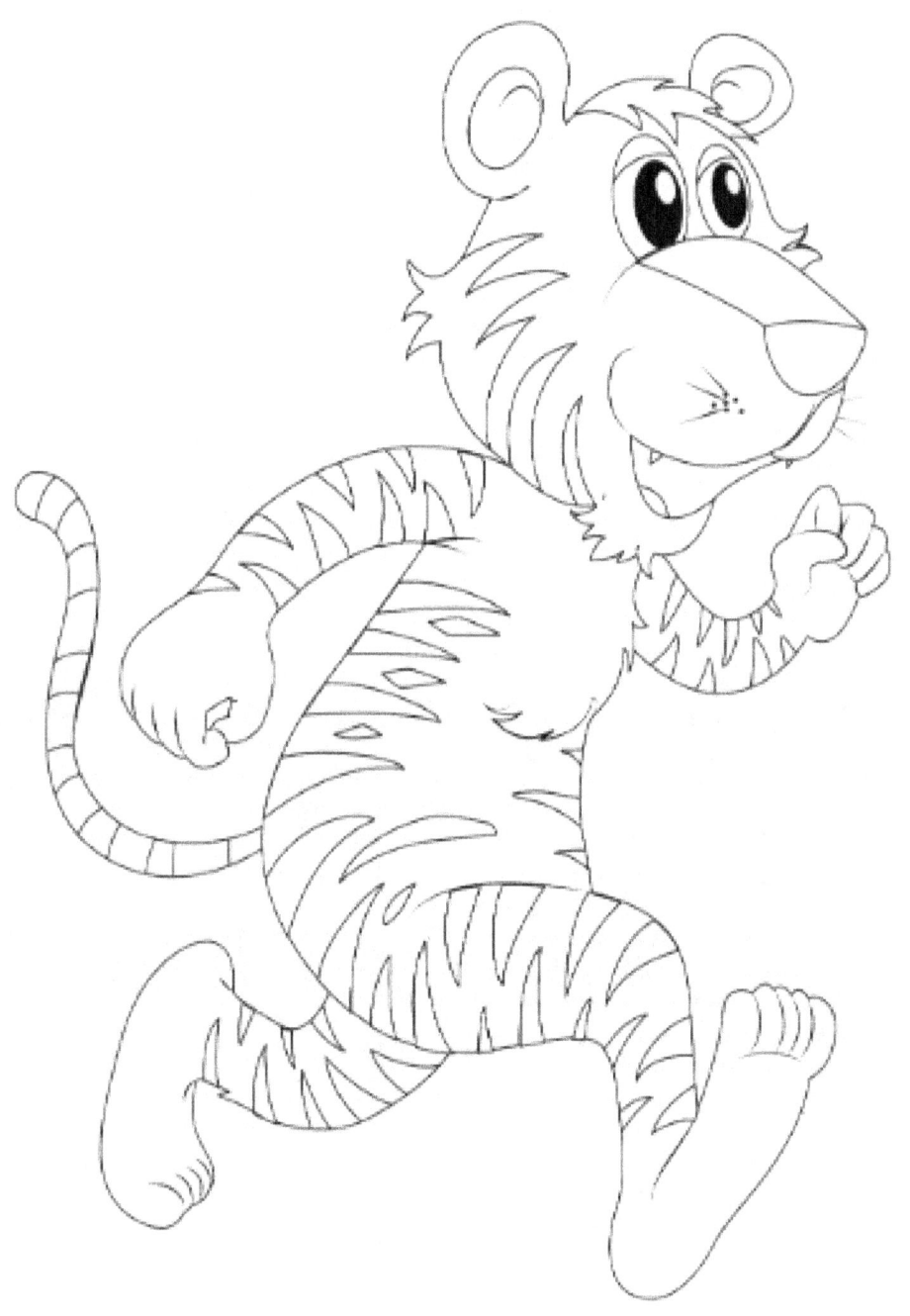

23

Twentythree

Squirrel

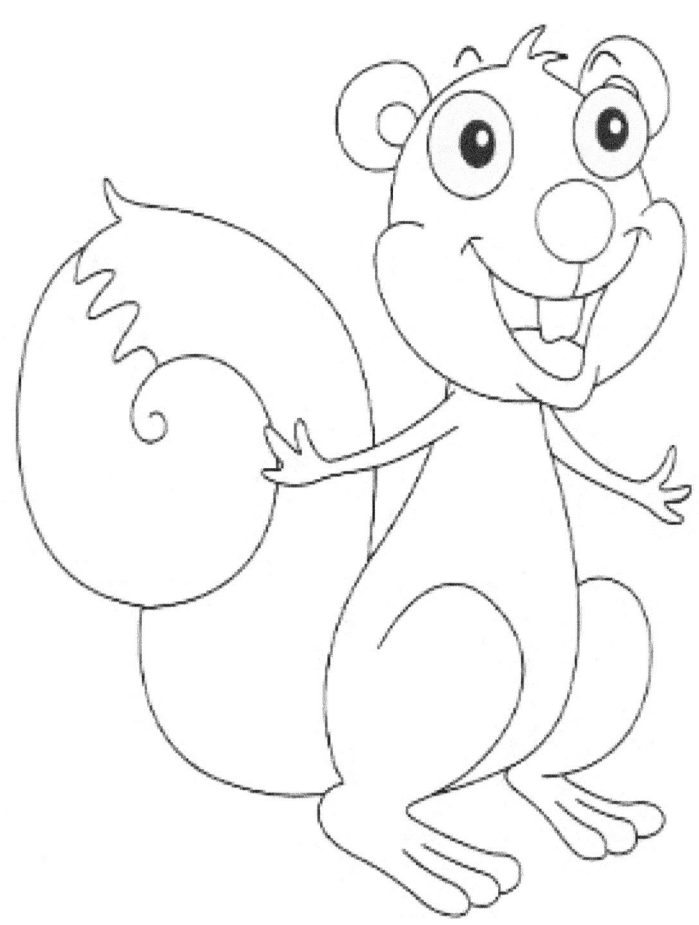

24

Twentyfour

Zebra

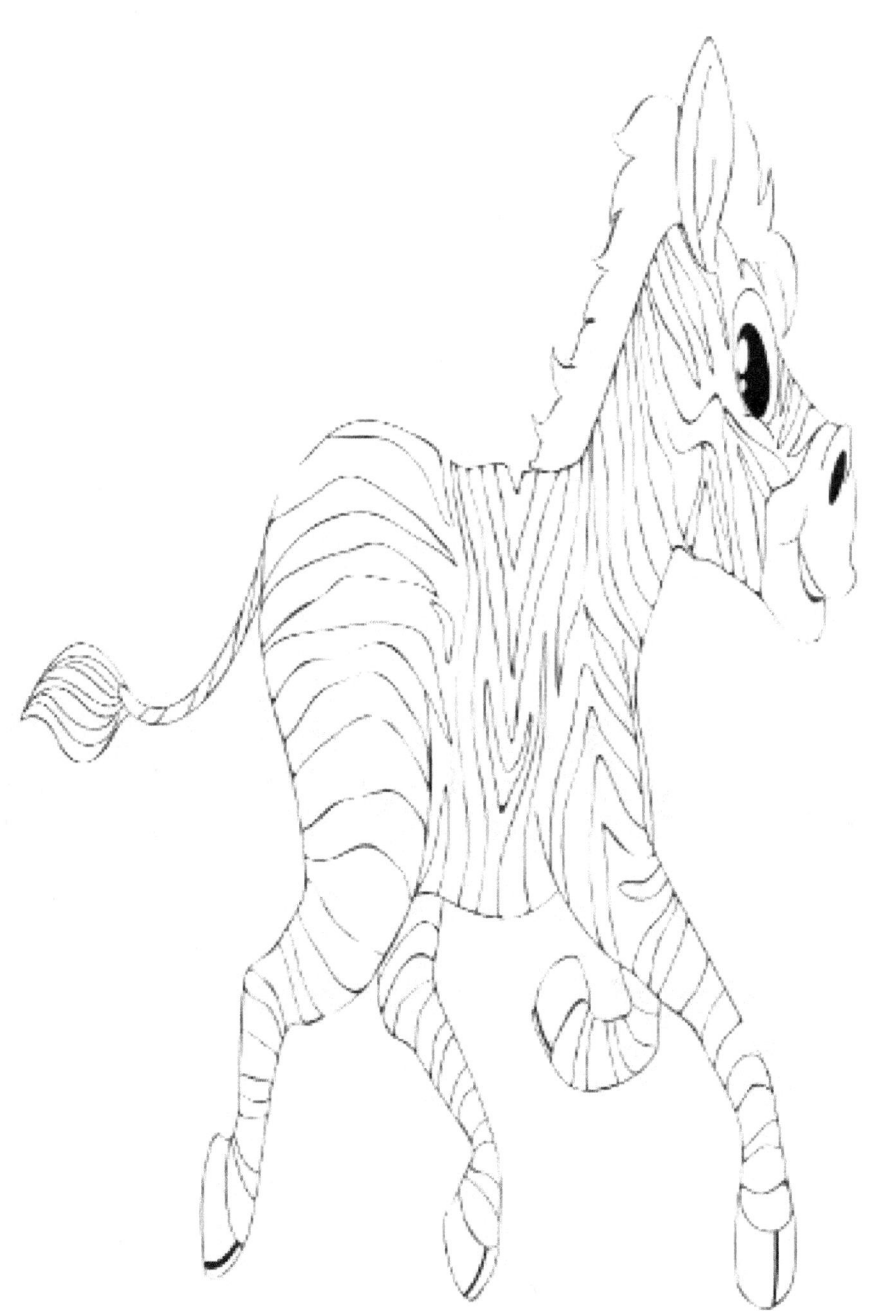

25

Twentyfive